G K S m Z V R W S e H O N A

I'm Going To READ!™

WORD FAMILIES

Rhyming Words

STERLING CHILDREN'S BOOKS
New York

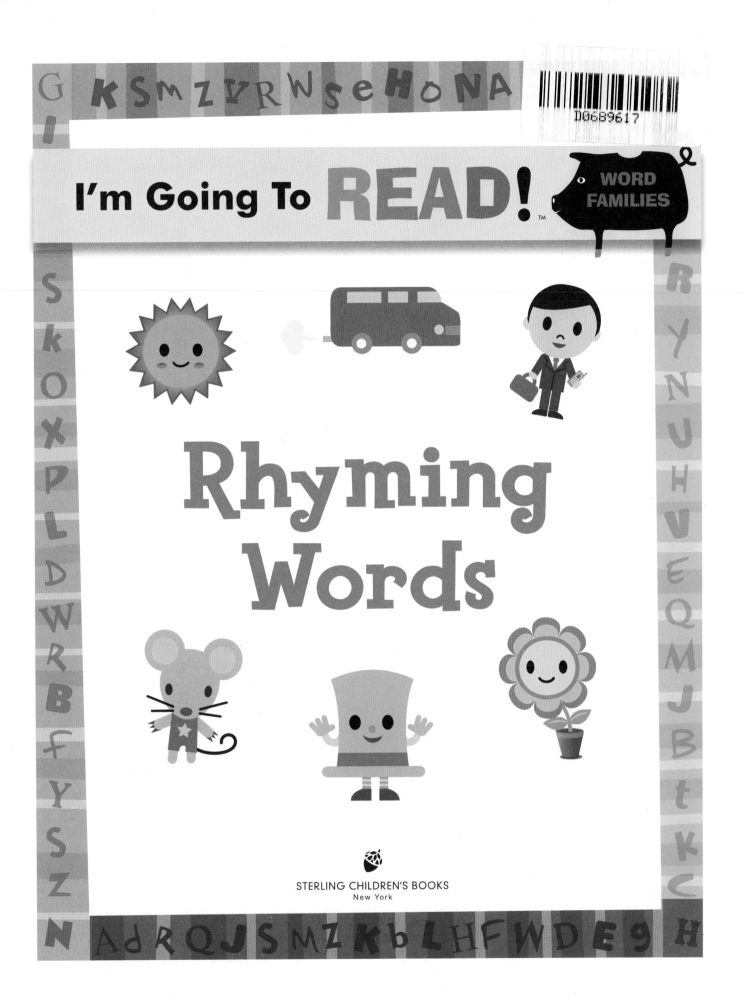

In this book you will learn to read these word families.

The ake Family

cake snake bake lake
rake flake shake

The an Family

man fan can
tan pan van

The ant Family

ant slant plant
chant pants

The at Family

bat cat hat
rat mat

The ate Family

crate gate skate
plate date late

The eet Family

beet feet meet
tweet sweet street

The ig Family

pig wig jig
dig big fig

The oat Family

oat float boat
coat moat goat

The op Family

stop pop top
cop shop hop

The ow Family

bow row crow
throw snow show

The ug Family

bug hug mug
rug plug jug

The un Family

sun fun bun run

The (ake) Family

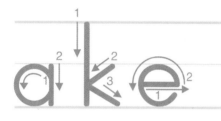

cake

Trace and write.

r

rake

b

bake

sn

snake

Write words that rhyme with cake.

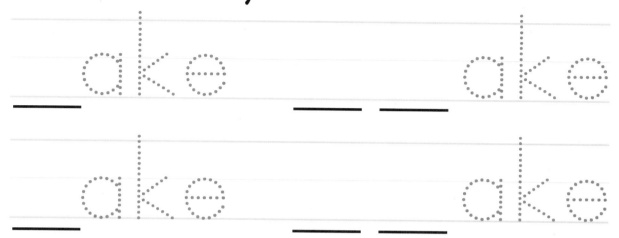

_ _ake   _ _ _ake

_ _ake   _ _ _ake

Write a sentence using words from the **ake** family.

flake

shake

Circle the words that end with **ake**.

bake

snake

plant

crow

lake

tweet

Write a rhyme using words that end with **ake**.

REVIEW

The **ake** Family

Fill in the letters.

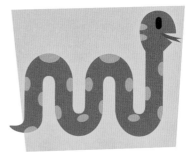

____ ____ ____ ____

____ ____ ____

____ ____ ____

____ ____ ____

____ ____ ____ ____

The **an** Family

man

Trace and write.

a n

an

man

can

c

fan

f

tan

t

can

fan

tan

Write words that rhyme with man.

___ an   ___ an

___ an   ___ an

Write a sentence using words from the **an** family.

van   pan

Circle the words that end with **an** .

van

plug

pan

pig

moat

fan

Write a rhyme using words that end with **an** .

REVIEW

The  **an** Family

Fill in the letters.

— — —

— — —

— — —

— — —

— — —

The ant Family

ant

Trace and write.

plant

p l

slant

s l

pants

p   s

plant

slant

pants

Write words that rhyme with ant.

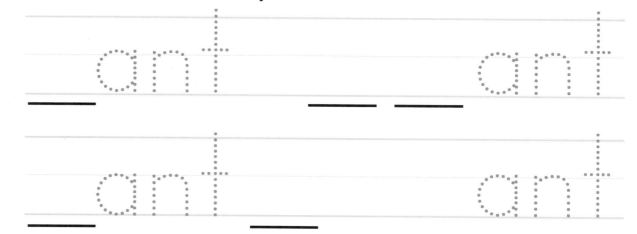

____ ant   ___ ___ ant

____ ant   ___ ant

Write a sentence using words from the **ant** family.

chant

pants

Circle the words that end with **ant** .

plant

stop

hug

slant

gate

sun

Write a rhyme using words that end with **ant** .

The **ant** Family

Fill in the letters.

ant

___ ___ ___

__ __ __ __ __

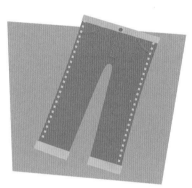

__ __ __ __ __

__ __ __ __

The at Family

hat

Trace and write.

cat

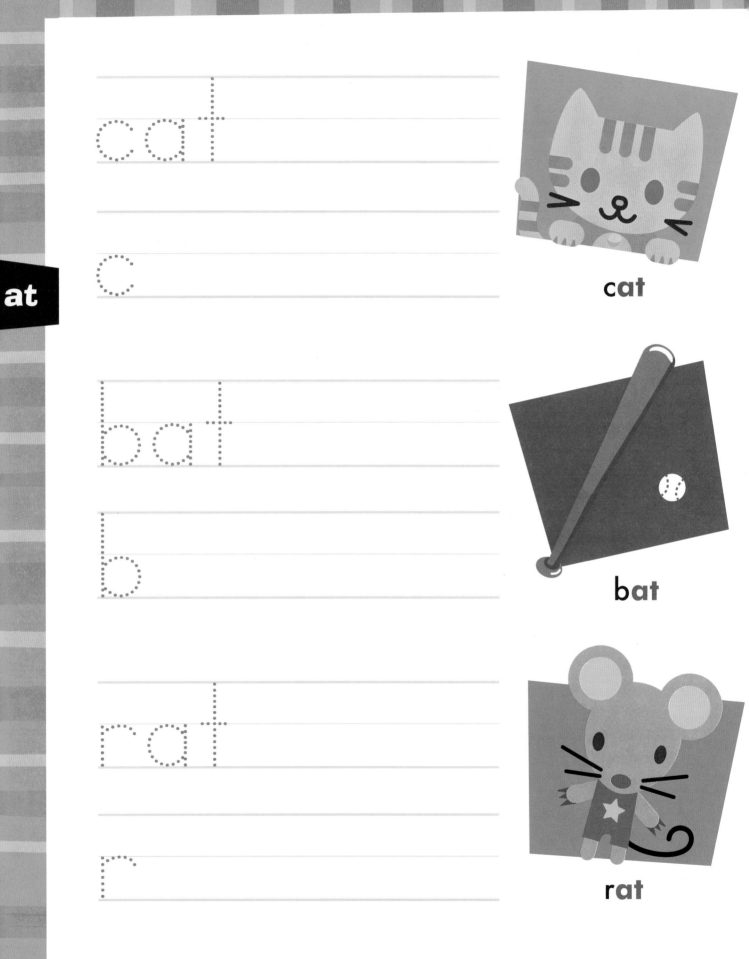

cat

bat

bat

rat

rat

Write words that rhyme with hat.

___ at   ___ at

___ at   ___ at

Write a sentence using words from the **at** family.

_____

_____

_____

_____

mat   **bat**

Circle the words that end with at.

cat

snow

rat

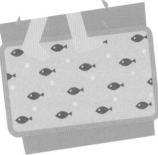
mat

fig

shake

Write a rhyme using words that end with **at**.

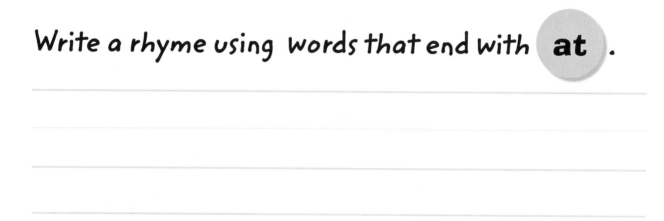

The (at) Family

Fill in the letters.

_ _ _ _

_ _ _ _

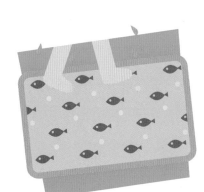

_ _ _

_ _ _

_ _ _

The ate Family

gate

Trace and write.

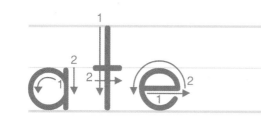

ate

gate

plate

pl

late

l

skate

sk

plate

late

skate

Write words that rhyme with gate.

_____ ate   _____ ate

_____ ate   _____ ate

Write a sentence using words from the **ate** family.

_____

_____

_____

_____

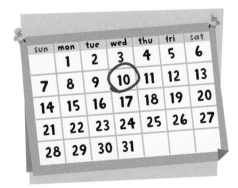

date

crate

Circle the words that end with **ate** .

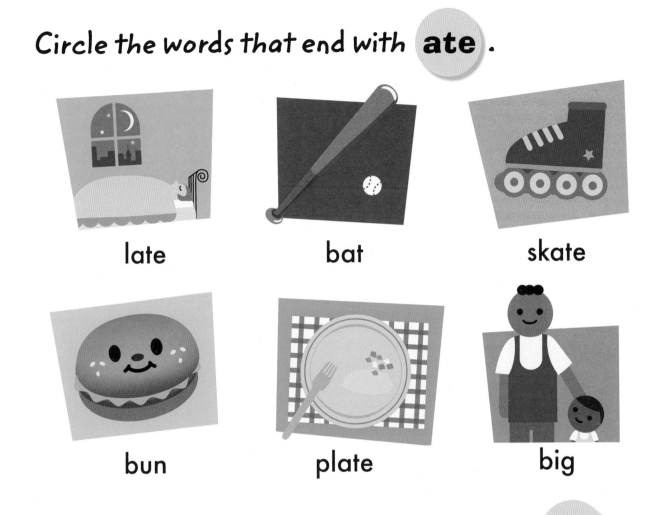

late

bat

skate

bun

plate

big

Write a rhyme using words that end with **ate** .

REVIEW

The (ate) Family

Fill in the letters.

_ _ _ _ _

ate

_ _ _ _ _ _ _

_ _ _ _ _

_ _ _ _ _

_ _ _ _ _

The  eet Family

feet

Trace and write.

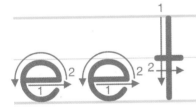

beet

b

meet

m

sweet

s

beet

meet

sweet

Write words that rhyme with feet.

___ ___ ___

___ ___ ___

Write a sentence using words from the eet family.

_____

_____

_____

_____

_____

street   tweet

Circle the words that end with **eet**.

pants   tweet   snake

sweet   bow   street

eet

Write a rhyme using words that end with **eet**.

REVIEW

The **eet** Family

Fill in the letters.

— — — — — —

— — — — — — —

— — — — — —

— — — — —

The ig Family

pig

Trace and write.

ig

i g

i g

p i g

jig
j

wig
w

dig
d

jig

wig

dig

Write words that rhyme with pig.

_ _ ig   _ _ ig

_ _ ig   _ _ ig

Write a sentence using words
from the **ig** family.

big   **fig**

ig

Circle the words that end with ig .

tan

mug

jig

cop

pig

date

Write a rhyme using words that end with ig .

REVIEW

The  ig Family

Fill in the letters.

_ _ _ _

_ _ _ _

_ _ _ _

_ _ _

_ _ _

ig

The (oat) Family

boat

Trace and write.

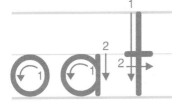

oat

boat

float

f

goat

g

coat

c

float

goat

coat

Write words that rhyme with boat.

_____ oat   _____ oat

_____ oat   _____ oat

Write a sentence using words from the **oat** family.

_____

_____

_____

_____

moat   **oat**

Circle the words that end with **oat** .

goat

coat

bug

beet

bat

float

Write a rhyme using words that end with **oat** .

The **oat** Family

Fill in the letters.

_ _ _ _ _

_ _ _ _ _

_ _ _ _ _

_ _ _ _ _

The op Family

pop

Trace and write.

op

pop

top

cop

hop

top

cop

hop

Write words that rhyme with pop.

___ op   ___ op

___ op   ___ ___ op

Write a sentence using words
from the **op** family.

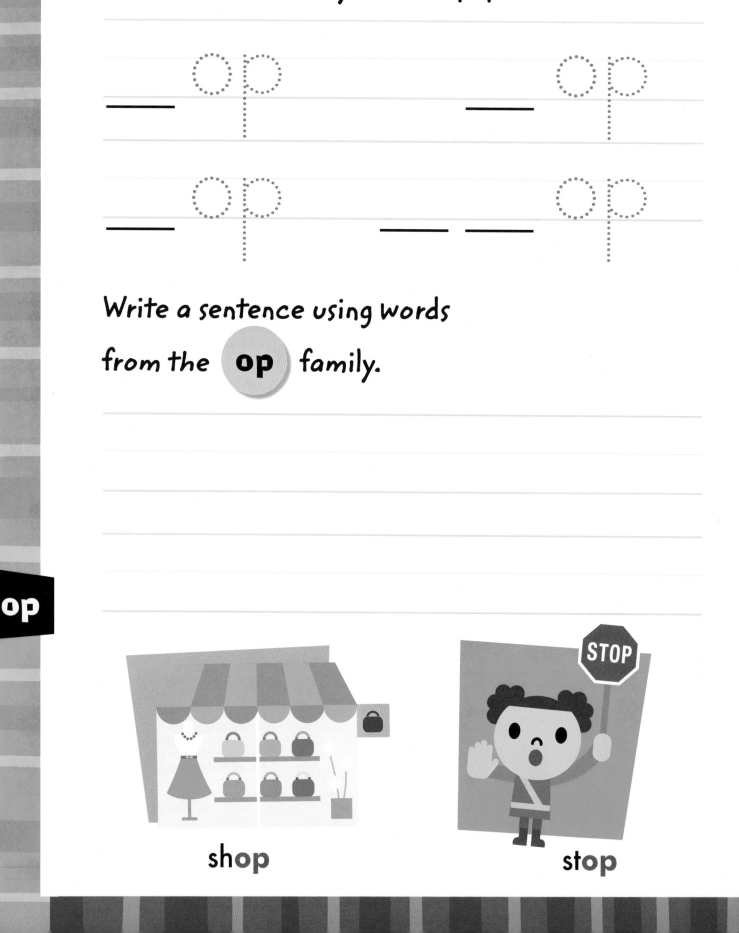

shop   stop

Circle the words that end with **op** .

crow

top

bat

dig

hop

stop

Write a rhyme using words that end with **op** .

REVIEW

The op Family

Fill in the letters.

_ _ _ _

_ _ _

op

_ _ _

_ _ _

_ _ _ _

The **ow** Family

row

Trace and write.

ow

row

bow

b

crow

cr

show

sh

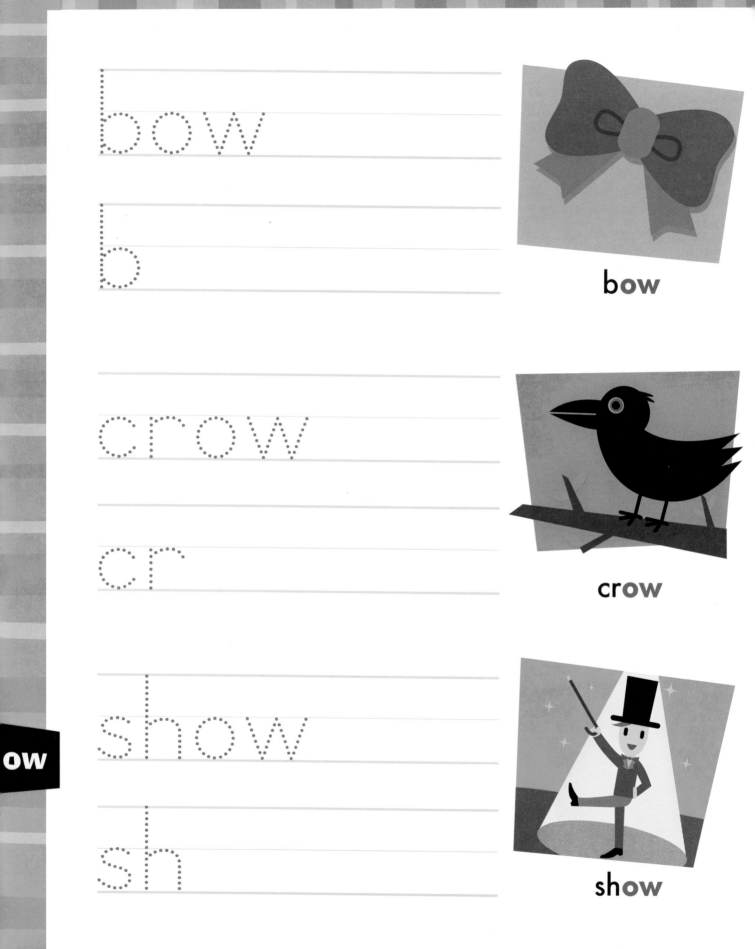

bow

crow

show

Write words that rhyme with row.

___ ow   ___ ___ ow

___ ow   ___ ___ ow

Write a sentence using words from the **ow** family.

throw   **snow**

Circle the words that end with **ow** .

bow

wig

rake

crow

can

snow

Write a rhyme using words that end with **ow** .

The (OW) Family

Fill in the letters.

_ _ _ _ _ _

_ _ _ _

_ _ _ _ _

_ _ _ _

_ _ _ _ _

The ug Family

bug

Trace and write.

ug

ug

bug

mug

m

hug

h

rug

r

mug

hug

rug

Write words that rhyme with bug.

___ug   ___ug

___ug   _____ug

Write a sentence using words from the **ug** family.

plug   jug

Circle the words that end with **ug** .

bug

crate

hug

oat

mug

shop

Write a rhyme using words that end with **ug** .

REVIEW

The (ug) Family

Fill in the letters.

_ _ _

_ _ _

_ _ _ _

_ _ _

_ _ _

The un Family

sun

Trace and write.

bun

b

run

r

fun

f

bun

run

fun

Write words that rhyme with sun.

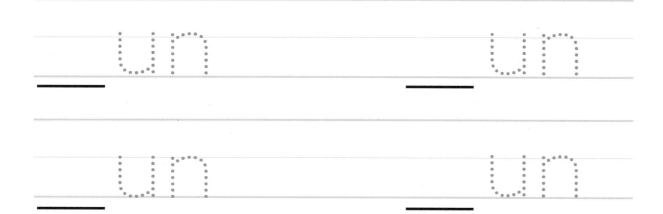

_ _ un   _ _ un

_ _ un   _ _ un

Write a sentence using words from the **un** family.

sun

Circle the words that end with **un** .

fun

hat

run

flake

bun

meet

Write a rhyme using words that end with **un** .

un

The **un** Family

Fill in the letters.

___ ___ ___

___ ___ ___

___ ___ ___

___ ___ ___

GREAT JOB!

_____
_____
_____

date

_____
_____
_____

first name

_____
_____

last name

K S m Z V R W S e H O N A S C D h

★ **I Can READ Rhyming Words**